EXPLORERS

Hernando de
Soto

Kristin Petrie

ABDO
Publishing Company

RAP 867 6027

visit us at
www.abdopub.com

Published by ABDO Publishing Company, 4940 Viking Drive, Edina, Minnesota 55435.
Copyright © 2004 by Abdo Consulting Group, Inc. International copyrights reserved in all
countries. No part of this book may be reproduced in any form without written permission from
the publisher.

Printed in the United States.

Cover Photos: Corbis
Interior Photos: Corbis pp. 5, 7, 9, 10, 11, 14, 15, 17, 18, 23, 27, 28, 29; North Wind pp. 13, 25

Series Coordinator: Stephanie Hedlund
Editors: Kate A. Conley, Kristin Van Cleaf
Art Direction & Cover Design: Neil Klinepier
Interior Design & Maps: Dave Bullen

Library of Congress Cataloging-in-Publication Data

Petrie, Kristin, 1970-
    Hernando De Soto / Kristin Petrie.
        p. cm. -- (Explorers)
    Includes index.
    Summary: A biography of the sixteenth-century Spaniard who explored Florida and other
southern states, and became the first white man to cross the Mississippi River.
    ISBN 1-59197-600-6
    1. Soto, Hernando de, ca. 1500-1542--Juvenile literature. 2. Explorers--America--Biography--
Juvenile literature. 3. Explorers--Spain--Biography--Juvenile literature. 4. America--Discovery
and exploration--Spanish--Juvenile literature. [1. De Soto, Hernando, ca. 1500-1542. 2.
Explorers. 3. America--Discovery and exploration--Spanish.] I. Title.

E125.S7P48 2004
970.01'6'092--dc22
    [B]   2003062925

970.016092
PET

Contents

Hernando de Soto

Hernando de Soto was born into an **era** of exploration. His heroes were brave men who explored foreign lands. They returned to Spain with stories, gold, and respect. De Soto would do the same.

De Soto accomplished many things for Spain. He helped take over the Inca Empire. Later, he led an expedition through more than 4,000 miles (6,400 km) of North America. De Soto and his army crossed several of today's southern states and the Mississippi River.

De Soto was sent to La Florida to explore as well as to establish Spanish colonies. He was also sent to convert the natives to Christianity. De Soto's personal mission was to find gold and glory.

1451
Christopher Columbus born

1485
Hernán Cortés born

1450
John Cabot born

1460
Vasco da Gama born

1491
Jacques Cartier born

Hernando de Soto was determined and fearless. He helped conquer the New World for Spain. Unfortunately, greed and cruelty marked many Spanish explorations, including de Soto's. And, Spain's growing empire caused the loss of the natives' way of life.

Hernando de Soto was a conquistador. Conquistadors were Spanish leaders and conquerors.

1492
Columbus's first voyage west for Spain

1496
Cabot's first voyage for England

1493
Columbus's second voyage, attempted to colonize Hispaniola

Early Life

Hernando de Soto was born in 1496 or 1497. Hernando's parents were Francisco Méndez de Soto and Leonor Arias Tinoco. They were minor nobility.

Hernando had an older brother, Juan, and two sisters named Catalina and María. The de Soto family lived in Jerez de los Caballeros, a town in southwestern Spain.

Little is known about Hernando's early life. However, it is known that he could read and write. He also knew some Latin and mathematics. So, Hernando probably attended school or was tutored by local priests.

Hernando was also influenced by stories of exploration and discovery. When the de Soto children were young, their neighbor traveled to the New World. His name was Vasco Núñez de Balboa.

1497
Cabot's second voyage, discovered the Grand Banks; da Gama was first to sail around Africa to India

1496 or 1497
Hernando de Soto born

1498
Cabot's third voyage, may have died; Columbus's third voyage

Balboa was the first Spaniard to gaze upon the Pacific Ocean. Around the same time, Spaniard Juan Ponce de León discovered land north of Cuba. He was the first Spaniard to see present-day Florida.

In 1513, Juan Ponce de León began his search for the mythical fountain of youth. During his search, he discovered Florida.

Would You?

Would you be inspired to explore if you had neighbors like Balboa and Ponce de León? What other explorers inspire you?

1502
Columbus's fourth voyage; da Gama's second voyage

1506
Columbus died

1504
Cortés sailed to the West Indies

First Travels

Hernando wished to follow in these Spaniards' footsteps. In 1514, the teenager left his family and moved to Seville, Spain. He became a soldier under the command of Pedro Arias Dávila.

Arias Dávila was made governor of a new colony called Darién in Central America. Hernando sailed with his commander to the New World. After crossing the Atlantic Ocean, Hernando explored the rain forests of Central America.

Natives in the New World feared the Spaniards and their weapons. For this reason, Hernando easily led troops in raids against them. The Spaniards killed many natives and enslaved others. Hernando became known for his bravery and his daring attacks.

Hernando's reputation as a dedicated soldier and excellent **cavalryman** grew. He continued to lead bold attacks. He was getting rich from **conquests** over native nations. Soon, he would be called to even more important positions.

1511
Cortés helped take over Cuba

**The old quarter
of Seville, Spain**

Wealthy Nations

In other parts of the New World, Spaniards made other **conquests**. De Soto wished to join the ranks of men such as Hernán Cortés. Cortés had conquered the mighty Aztec Nation in 1521. He had seized huge amounts of gold and silver, making him a very wealthy man.

De Soto soon became involved in a new mission. In 1527, Spaniard Francisco Pizarro captured a number of natives off the coast of South America. The natives were of the Incan tribe, which was highly civilized and as powerful as the Aztecs.

The Inca Empire was huge! It stretched more than 2,000 miles (3,200 km) down the west coast of South America. The empire extended

Francisco Pizarro

1524
Da Gama's third voyage, died in Cochin, India

1519–1521
Cortés conquered the Aztec Empire and claimed Mexico for Spain

1532
De Soto helped attack the Inca Empire

into the Andes Mountains in the interior of the continent. Pizarro believed great wealth awaited him in this empire.

King Charles I of Spain granted Pizarro **permission** to attack the Inca Empire in 1529. Hernando de Soto then became involved in the **conquest**. De Soto was already rich from other victories, so he lent Pizarro two ships. De Soto joined Pizarro when gold was found.

King Charles I
of Spain

Would You?

Would you want to join in the search for riches? What do you think you would look for?

The Incas

Pizarro had assembled an army of 180 men and 37 horses. De Soto joined him at Puná, in what is now Peru, with another 100 men and 25 horses. Because of his contributions, de Soto was made second in command.

De Soto led the Spaniards' most powerful weapon, the horsemen. Natives of the New World feared horses. They had never seen such large beasts before and often ran at the sight of them.

The army left Puná in the early months of 1532. The soldiers began their journey south. Along the way, Pizarro and de Soto learned of a war taking place among the Incas.

Five years earlier, the king of the Inca Empire had died. His two sons were fighting over who would rule the kingdom. This information pleased the Spaniards. Disagreement among the tribes would make it easier to conquer the empire. They continued on their expedition.

1534
Cartier's first voyage for France

1539–1542
De Soto explored La Florida

1533
De Soto helped take over Cuzco

1535
Cartier's second voyage

In October, an Incan ambassador requested a peaceful meeting with the Spaniards. Pizarro agreed to meet with him. After exchanging gifts, the ambassador suggested the Spaniards continue on their journey. They would soon meet Atahuallpa, one of the king's sons.

Pizarro's expedition included more than 50 horses. Spaniards used the horses to conquer the natives.

At Cajamarca

Pizarro and de Soto led their troops across desert and mountains. Finally, they reached the Incan city of Cajamarca. There, the new Incan king Atahuallpa and an army of 30,000 warriors waited for the Spaniards.

Atahuallpa

The Spanish army was down to 168 soldiers. However, Pizarro and de Soto did not want to show fear of the huge Incan army. So despite being outnumbered, the Spaniards marched past the Incan troops.

On November 15, 1532, Pizarro sent de Soto to meet Atahuallpa. De Soto wanted to make the Incan ruler fear him. To do this, the Spaniard rode so close to Atahuallpa that his horse breathed on the king. Despite this, Atahuallpa barely acknowledged de Soto!

Ruins of Incan cities such as Machu Picchu can be found in Peru.

Early Native Americans

●●●

About 30,000 years ago, the first people immigrated to North and South America from Asia. They crossed the Bering Strait land bridge and spread throughout the land.

In the 1500s, Europeans came to the New World. They were often outnumbered by the Native Americans, just as Pizarro and de Soto were in Cajamarca. However, the Europeans' animals, advanced weapons, and deadly diseases cost thousands of natives their lives.

1547
Cortés died

1557
Cartier died

1542
Coronado returned to New Spain; de Soto died

1554
Coronado died

1566
Drake's first voyage to the New World

However, Atahuallpa was soon impressed when de Soto demonstrated his horsemanship and bravery. Because of this, Atahuallpa invited Pizarro to visit the next day. Meanwhile, Pizarro had made a plan to take Atahuallpa **hostage**.

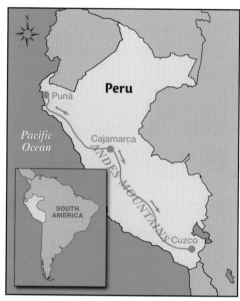

Pizarro and de Soto's route to conquer the Incas

The plan went exactly as Pizarro expected. Early on November 16, the Spanish soldiers hid in the abandoned buildings of Cajamarca. Later that day, the Incan king entered the city with an escort of unarmed Incas.

Pizarro sent a priest to meet him. Then at a signal from the priest, the Spaniards attacked from all sides. In a short time, the Incan ruler was captured.

The battle lasted the rest of the day, and about 7,000 Incas died. In the following weeks, the Incas collected a large **ransom** of gold and silver for their ruler's release. Pizarro took the ransom but killed Atahuallpa anyway.

1567
Drake's second voyage

1577
Drake began a worldwide voyage, was first Englishman to sail the Pacific Ocean

1570 and 1572
Drake terrorized the Spanish in the New World

Would you believe you could win a battle with 168 soldiers against 30,000 warriors? How do you think the Spaniards felt before the battle?

Pizarro's capture of Atahuallpa

In Charge

The ruins of Cuzco

At the end of November 1533, the Spanish army took over the Incan capital of Cuzco. The next year, Pizarro named de Soto lieutenant governor of the city. Pizarro also divided up the Incas' wealth. De Soto received a portion of the Incas' gold and silver.

Hernando de Soto was now one of the richest men in Spain's empire. He returned to Spain in 1536. There, he married a woman named Isabel de Bobadillo.

1588
Drake helped England win the Battle of Gravelines against Spain's Invincible Armada

1581
Drake knighted by Queen Elizabeth I

1596
Drake died

Isabel was the daughter of de Soto's past commander, Pedro Arias Dávila. The de Sotos lived in a luxurious home in Seville.

De Soto, however, was restless. Despite his successes, he'd always been second in command. He wanted to be in charge and to receive all the glory for a new **conquest**. He also wanted to search for more treasure.

Spain's king Charles I granted de Soto an expedition to explore the land north of Cuba. It was called La Florida. On April 7, 1538, the expedition set sail from Sanlúcar de Barrameda, Spain. This time, de Soto was first in command of 10 ships, 700 men, and 250 horses.

Would You?

Would you want to be in charge of an expedition? What do you think de Soto said to convince King Charles I?

1728
James Cook born

1765
Boone journeyed to Florida

1768
Cook sailed for Tahiti

1734
Daniel Boone born

1767
Boone explored Kentucky

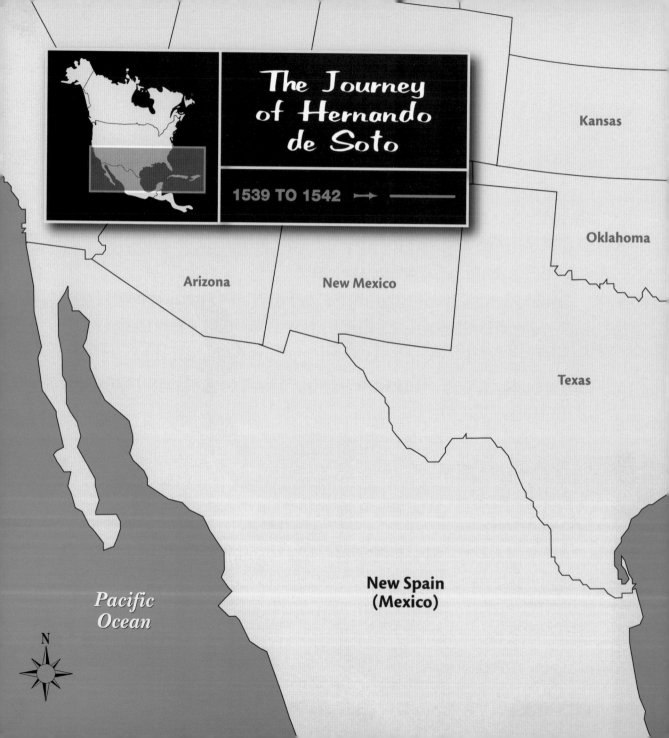

The Journey
of Hernando
de Soto

1539 TO 1542 →

Kansas

Oklahoma

Arizona

New Mexico

Texas

New Spain
(Mexico)

Pacific
Ocean

N

Illinois

Indiana

Ohio

Missouri

Mississippi River

Kentucky

West Virginia

Virginia

North Carolina

APPALACHIAN MOUNTAINS

Arkansas

Tennessee

Cofitachequi

South Carolina

Savannah River

Alabama

Georgia

Atlantic Ocean

Mississippi

Louisiana

Mobile

Anhaica

La Florida

Ocita

Ocale

Tampa Bay

Gulf of Mexico

Cuba

Caribbean Sea

La Florida

The **fleet** first stopped at Cuba to prepare for the expedition. In May 1539, de Soto's crew sailed from Cuba to the shores of La Florida. They landed near today's Tampa Bay.

Shortly after their landing, the expedition met a Spaniard named Juan Ortiz. In 1528, Ortiz had been separated from an expedition led by Pánfilo de Narváez. Since that time, Ortiz had lived with a native tribe. So, he knew the native language and **customs**. He became an interpreter for de Soto.

De Soto settled his army in an abandoned village called Ocita. From there, de Soto sent scouts in search of information about the region. They found no riches in the area. However, they heard rumors about a wealthy nation called Ocale to the northeast.

De Soto led his soldiers northeast through rain and swamps. The men reached Ocale, but found no gold. The

Spaniards stole the natives' food and other supplies. To get rid of the **intruders**, the natives said another village to the north might contain gold.

Spaniards discover Juan Ortiz living with the natives.

1778
Cook became the first European to record Hawaiian Islands; Boone captured by Shawnee

1775
Boone cut the Wilderness Road from Virginia to Kentucky

1779
Cook died

Cofitachequi

De Soto reached the Apalachee Nation's capital, Anhaica, in October 1539. He found no gold there, either. However, food was plentiful. De Soto and his army stayed in Anhaica for the winter.

During their stay, the Spaniards were told about a wealthy city near the rising sun. Can you imagine chasing the rising sun? The natives had figured out how to get rid of the Spaniards. They told one tale after another about imaginary cities filled with gold.

De Soto led his army to the north in the spring of 1540. The journey took the army through the wilderness of present-day Georgia and South Carolina. On May 1, 1540, the soldiers reached the city of Cofitachequi, near the Savannah River.

The natives' ruler, the Lady of Cofitachequi, was kind and generous. She provided the army with food and housing.

1813
John C. Frémont born

1842
Frémont's first independent surveying mission

1820
Boone died

Her people gave the Spaniards pearls and copper. Many soldiers wanted to settle there, but de Soto pressed on. He believed gold and glory were still to be found.

The Lady of Cofitachequi greeted de Soto with pearls.

Pushing On

De Soto took the Lady of Cofitachequi **hostage** and left the area. The expedition eventually crossed the Appalachian Mountains. Then, it turned north and reached what is now Tennessee. Next, de Soto led his men south again.

In October 1540, de Soto neared present-day Mobile, Alabama. Thousands of Native Americans **ambushed** the Spaniards. By the end of the battle, about 2,500 natives had died. De Soto claimed victory. But, he had lost men, horses, and much of the army's **ammunition** and food.

Nevertheless, Hernando de Soto pushed on. He led the troops back to the north. They spent the winter of 1540 in the region of the Chickasaw Nation. There, the Spaniards were often attacked by the natives.

De Soto emerged victorious from these attacks as well. However, he lost more men and horses. His remaining

1856
Frémont ran for president of the United States but lost

1845-1846
Frémont explored the Great Basin and the Pacific Coast, fought in the Mexican War

1890
Frémont died

soldiers were injured and hungry. What was de Soto to do? The relentless commander turned west.

In May 1541, the troops reached the Mississippi River. For one month, the soldiers worked to make four large, flat boats. They used them to cross the river. De Soto then led his men through today's Arkansas and Louisiana.

De Soto was the first European to cross the Mississippi River.

1910
Jacques Cousteau born

1951
Cousteau's first expedition in the Red Sea

1942
Cousteau and Gagnan developed the Aqua-Lung for diving

Last Days

In March 1542, de Soto decided to return to the Mississippi River. He planned to travel down the river to the Gulf of Mexico. There, he would establish a colony and send for **reinforcements**. De Soto had finally admitted defeat.

By the time the troops reached the river, de Soto was very sick. He named Luis Moscoso the new leader of the expedition. Hernando de Soto died on May 21, 1542.

Hernando de Soto

The Spanish troops knew that without de Soto they would be easily overcome. They buried de Soto's body in the Mississippi so the natives wouldn't know he had died.

With de Soto's death, the expedition ended. Moscoso led the 311 remaining soldiers to Mexico in September 1543. The expedition had lasted more than four years.

De Soto's determined march through today's southern United States accomplished much for Spain. The country then focused on the land's other resources, such as the Mississippi River, for wealth. Spanish colonization soon began in La Florida.

De Soto's burial in the Mississippi River

Glossary

ambush - a surprise attack from a hidden position.

ammunition - bullets, shells, and other items used in firearms.

cavalryman - a member of a branch of an army consisting of soldiers who fight on horseback.

conquest - the act of conquering.

customs - the habits of a group that are passed on through generations.

era - a period of time or history.

fleet - a group of ships under one command.

hostage - a person held captive by another person or group in order to make a deal with authorities.

intruder - a person who enters an area, such as another person's home, without permission.

permission - formal consent.

ransom - money demanded for the release of a captive.

reinforcements - the addition of soldiers to strengthen an army.

Saying It

Appalachian - ah-puh-LAY-chuhn
Atahuallpa - ah-tah-WAHL-pah
Cajamarca - kah-hah-MAHR-kah
Darién - dahr-YEHN
Jerez de los Caballeros - hay-REHTH thay lohs kah-bah-LYAY-rohs
Pánfilo de Narváez - PAHM-fee-loh thay nahr-BAH-ayth
Sanlúcar de Barrameda - sahn-LOO-kahr thay bah-rah-MAY-thah
Vasco Núñez de Balboa - VAHS-koh NOON-yayth thay bahl-BOH-uh

Web Sites

To learn more about Hernando de Soto, visit ABDO Publishing Company on the World Wide Web at **www.abdopub.com**. Web sites about Hernando de Soto are featured on our Book Links page. These links are routinely monitored and updated to provide the most current information available.

Index